THE *fullness* OF THE
HOLY SPIRIT

THE fullness OF THE HOLY SPIRIT

BOB YANDIAN

Whitaker House

Unless otherwise indicated, all Scripture quotations are taken from the *King James Version* (KJV) of the Bible.

THE FULLNESS OF THE HOLY SPIRIT

Bob Yandian
Bob Yandian Ministries
P.O. Box 55236
Tulsa, OK 74155-1236

ISBN: 0-88368-357-1
Printed in the United States of America
Copyright © 1982, 1987 by Bob Yandian

Whitaker House
580 Pittsburgh Street
Springdale, PA 15144

1 2 3 4 5 6 7 8 9 10 11 12 / 05 04 03 02 01 00 99 98 97 96 95

Contents

Foreword

In his book, eloquent Bible teacher Bob Yandian traces the vital works of the Holy Spirit from the fall of Adam and Eve through the present time, showing the necessity of every believer's receiving the baptism in the Holy Spirit after receiving the experience of the New Birth.

Bob's careful examination of oil and wine in scripture leads him to a penetrating study of the story of the Good Samaritan — including a clue as to the time of the Lord's return.

Bob also takes up such challenging questions as: Did Adam die spiritually? Does a person need to speak in tongues? Can a person interpret what he prays in tongues? Does the devil understand what you pray in tongues?

Bob was an employee of our ministry for a number of years. After diligent study in the Word, he became an instructor at our Rhema Bible Training Center for several more years, and later became pastor of Grace Fellowship in Tulsa. We rejoice at how God has been blessing his life in his new position. It is a pleasure to recommend his new book to you for your thoughtful study.

Kenneth E. Hagin

Introduction

The last half of Mark 16 is under controversy today. Many people believe the last part of this chapter has been added. They quote verse 15:

> Go ye into all the world, and preach the gospel to every creature.

But they end with that verse. Verses 17 and 18 go on to say:

> And these signs shall follow them that believe; In my name shall they cast out devils; they shall speak with new tongues;

> They shall take up serpents; and if they drink any deadly thing, it shall not hurt them; they shall lay hands on the sick, and they shall recover.

What I was surprised to find out was that the controversy was not over casting out devils (Jesus did this), taking up serpents or drinking deadly things and not being harmed (if Jesus had done this, He would not have been hurt), or laying hands on the sick and seeing them recover (Jesus did this also). The big controversy comes over speaking with new tongues probably because this is the *only* reference we find in the Bible that Jesus ever made to speaking with tongues.

The thrust of this book will be to show from many other scriptures that there is indeed more to the work of the Holy Spirit than just the New Birth. Jesus told us in the parable of the Good Samaritan that *oil* and *wine* were poured into the wounds of the man who was beaten and robbed. Reference to those two elements started me into a fascinating study in the Word of God of the two separate and distinct works of the Holy Spirit.

1
The Good Samaritan

In Luke 10:25-37, we read the parable of the good Samaritan presented by Jesus. This parable has been taught to us from early days in Sunday school as a model lesson of learning to love and help those who are down and out. This parable, like most, has more than just a surface meaning. In it, I find a representational picture of the time from the fall of Adam until the Second Coming of the Lord Jesus Christ.

The parable actually begins in verse 25 when the lawyer asked Jesus a tempting question of how to gain eternal life. One of the commandments which was necessary was *"love thy neighbour as thyself"* (Lev. 19:18). The parable of the Good Samaritan was given in response to the lawyer's question of *"who is my neighbour?"* (v. 29). Jesus replied in verse 30:

> . . . A certain man went down from Jerusalem to Jericho, and fell among thieves, which stripped him of his

raiment, and wounded him, and departed, leaving him half dead.

When Adam was placed here on the earth, he was given authority to rule and dominate this planet. He was the god of this world until Satan tricked him and took away his authority. Satan then became the god of this world after he brought in the curse. (See Gen. 1-3; Deut. 28:15-68.)

Notice that the man (Adam) fell among *thieves*. John 10:10 describes the thief which is *Satan*. Satan and his demons — "the *thieves*" of Luke 10:30 — did three things to this man. First, they stripped him of his raiment; second, they wounded him; and third, they departed leaving him half dead. This is the three-fold curse of the law: poverty ("*stripped him of his raiment*"), sickness ("*wounded him*"), and spiritual death ("*departed, leaving him half dead*").

It is significant that the man was left half dead; because, when Adam sinned in the Garden, he did not fall over dead even though God told him that if he ate of the fruit, he would surely die. (Gen. 2:17.) At the moment that Adam ate of the fruit, he died *spiritually*, but he was still alive *physically*. In other words, he was *half dead*.

And by chance there came down a certain priest that way: and when he saw him, he passed by on the other side.

And likewise a Levite, when he was at the place, came and looked on him, and passed by on the other side (vv. 31,32).

The *priest* and *Levite* both represent the law with its ritual and sacrifice. Notice that neither one could help, but had to pass by on the other side. The law was never designed to save man, but to tell man that he is a sinner and needs a savior. (See Rom. 3:20; 5:20; Gal. 3:19.)

Also notice that both passed *by chance*. The law would never have been introduced if man had accepted God's Word by faith. Abraham lived by faith and lived in the blessings and *never knew of the law*. Both the priest and Levite were repulsed by the sight of this man and passed by him.

VERSES 33,34

But a certain Samaritan, as he journeyed, came where he was: and when he saw him, he had compassion on him,

And went to him, and bound up his wounds, pouring in oil and wine, and set him on his own beast, and brought him to an inn, and took care of him.

Thank God for Jesus, Our Good Samaritan. He did not come by chance, but was on a journey with a definite purpose. He did not "pass by on the other side," but *came* to us. You did not have to go to Jesus, *He came to you.* When we were lost and dead in our trespasses and sin, Christ died for us.

The Samaritan also had *compassion* on the man and bound up his *wounds.* Notice, there is *healing* in the atoning work of Jesus. The second curse introduced by the thieves in verse 30 was the wounding of this man which represented the curse of sickness. Jesus died to redeem us from *sickness* as well as from sin. (See Ps. 103:3.) Jesus bound up our wounds. He did this by pouring in two elements — *oil* and *wine.* We will look at the meaning of oil and wine in detail within the next few pages.

Finally, the Good Samaritan brought this man to an inn and took care of him. The inn represents the Church. When Jesus redeemed you, He placed you into the Church, the Body of Christ, and turned you over to the innkeeper, the Holy Spirit, for safekeeping. *"And I will pray the Father, and he shall give you another Comforter, that he may abide with you for ever"* (John 14:16).

VERSE 35

And on the morrow when he departed, he took out two pence, and gave them to the host, and said unto him, Take care of him; and whatsoever thou spendest more, when I come again, I will repay thee.

Jesus told us that He is *coming again*. After He turned us over to the host, the Holy Spirit — the innkeeper — for our dispensation, He promised to come again for us. The disciples were told by two angels — men *"in white apparel"* — at the ascension of Jesus that Jesus would again come to earth in *"like manner as ye have seen him go into heaven"* (Acts 1:11). Jesus said in the closing of this parable:

Which now of these three, thinkest thou, was neighbour unto him that fell among the thieves?

And he [the lawyer] said, He that shewed mercy on him. Then said Jesus unto him, Go, and do thou likewise (vv. 36,37).

The original question in verse 29 was: ". . . *And who is my neighbour?*" In this particular parable, Jesus is not teaching a lesson about loving the down and outer (which we *should do*), but a lesson about loving *Him*, the neighbor who gives eternal life. Jesus teaches in other passages about loving others (Matt. 5:43-47), but not as a means of gaining salvation. The parable of the good Samaritan is different because it was given in response to a question of how to inherit eternal life. (v. 25.) *We* are the one in the road. Without Jesus we are helpless. Jesus was teaching that the way to gain eternal life was to *love Him*.

If you are without eternal life, the plan of salvation is very simple. Turn away from the priest and Levite (your own works, creeds, and doctrines) and realize your own helplessness. Look up to *Jesus*. He is the only One Who has something to offer you. He wants to give you the *oil* of the New Birth and the *wine* of the infilling of the Holy Spirit. Salvation is as simple as believing that God raised Jesus Christ from the dead, and confessing that Jesus is now the Lord of your life. (Rom. 10:9,10.) He will then deliver you safely to the inn and turn you over to the Holy Spirit for safekeeping until He comes back for you.

2
Oil and Wine

Just as in the parable of the good Samaritan, Jesus poured oil and wine into our wounds. Jesus did something for us that the law (priest and Levite) could not. The law had nothing to give, but Jesus did. The oil and wine are both representations of two of the major works of the Holy Spirit in the earth today during the church age.

The Holy Spirit has always been with man, but in a limited ministry before the day of Pentecost. In the Old Testament, the Holy Spirit lived in a temple made with hands. When Jesus Christ rose from the dead, the veil of the temple was rent from the top to the bottom. That was not just to let us in, but to let the Holy Spirit out. From that day, He has desired to live in us. He thinks we are more valuable than a temple which costs millions of dollars. Today *we* are His temple and He dwells, or lives, in us.

First Corinthians 3:16 says, *"Know ye not that ye (believers) are the temple of God, and that the Spirit of God dwelleth in you"*? (See also 1 Corinthians 6:19). Romans 8:11 tells us: *"But if the Spirit of him that raised up Jesus from the dead dwell in you, he that raised up Christ from the dead shall also quicken your mortal bodies by his Spirit that dwelleth in you."* Romans 8:11 also tells us that *divine healing* is for every member of the Body of Christ: *all* who are indwelled by the Holy Spirit. You do not have to be filled with the Holy Spirit to be healed. The work of the cross is for everyone.

In the Old Testament, the Holy Spirit did not live in those who were saints. He came *on* individuals at certain times to do certain tasks, but His ministry was limited. And just as the Holy Spirit could come on people, He would leave.

When the Holy Spirit came on him one day, Elijah girded up his loins and outran Ahab's chariot across the plains of Jezreel. (1 Kings 18.) Elijah could not run like that all the time, only when he was anointed. Just a few days later we find the same man running from the queen who sent him a threatening message. Elijah ran again, but this time he was not under the power of the Holy Spirit. He ran in his own strength, became exhausted, and sat down under a tree. (1 Kings 19.)

Samson was not strong twenty-four hours a day. He could do superhuman feats only when the "hand of the Lord" (the Holy Spirit) came on him.

No one in the Old Testament had the Holy Spirit dwelling in them, in their spirit. When a person under the Old Covenant came in contact with the Holy Spirit, he was in danger of being struck dead. The only way he could survive was to be anointed by the Spirit at that time. The priests who ministered for the people had to be anointed by the Holy Spirit so they would not die while in the Holy of Holies in the temple. (Exod. 28:35.) Tradition tells us that the priest had a rope tied to him, and if he entered the presence of the Lord with any unconfessed sin in his life he would be struck dead. The rope would then be used by the people to pull the priest back out, since they could not go in after him themselves.

Today, since the Spirit lives in us as believers, we could go back into that time period with no fear at all of the presence of God. We would simply walk into the Holy of Holies, past the veil, and pick up the ark of the covenant with boldness. We are God's children, in His family, and indwelled by His own Spirit.

The Holy Spirit came to live in us when we were born again. When we confessed Jesus as our Lord, and believed in our hearts that God raised Him from the dead, the Holy Spirit came and recreated our human spirit and made us His permanent home.

In the parable of the Good Samaritan, this is seen when the man (the Lord) poured *oil* into the wound *first*. OIL is a "type and shadow," representing something to come. Oil symbolizes the Holy Spirit in the New Birth. The *indwelling of* the Holy Spirit comes before the *infilling* (the wine). The new birth comes first: oil, *then* wine.

On the day of Pentecost, both the New Birth (oil) and the Infilling of the Holy Spirit (wine) were given. Not only was *wine* poured out on that day, but *oil* also. Many people had believed on the Lord before that day, but were not *born again* until the Holy Spirit was given. John 1:12 tells us, *"But as many as received him, to them gave he power to become the sons of God, even to them that believe on his name."* Those who believed on His name *became* the sons of God on the day of Pentecost. On the day of Pentecost those in the upper room received first the oil (they were born again), then they received the wine (they were filled and began to speak with new tongues).

Joel's prophecy, a portion of which was quoted by Peter on the day of Pentecost, says, *"And the floors shall be full of wheat, and the vats shall overflow with wine and oil . . . . And it shall come to pass afterward, that I will pour out my spirit upon all flesh; and your sons and your daughters shall prophesy, your old men shall dream dreams, your young men shall see visions. And also upon the servants and upon the hand-maids in those days will I pour out my spirit."* (Joel 2:24,28,29). The vats overflowed in heaven and spilled onto the earth that day, starting in an upper room in Jerusalem.

Oil and wine are used together throughout the Word of God to show the double blessing of the Holy Spirit. David said in Psalm 23:5, *". . . thou anointest my head with oil; my cup runneth over"* (analogy of filling with wine). Psalm 104:15 says, *"And wine that maketh glad the heart of man, and oil to make his face to shine . . . ."*

Spiritual Wineskins —

One of the most graphic uses of oil and wine in the Word is found in Matthew 9:17.

Jesus said, *"Neither do men put new wine into old bottles: else the bottles break, and the new wine runneth out, and the bottles perish: but they put new wine into new bottles, and both are preserved."*

In the time in which this was written, a "bottle" was a wineskin. Many of the different translations render the word *bottle* as "wineskin." Unless wine was kept in the wineskin at all times, the container would become hard and parched when left dry. Dried wineskins needed to be made soft again before wine could be poured in.

The Greek will give us some insight into this verse to help us learn exactly what Jesus was saying. There are two Greek words for "new." One is *neos* which means "brand new," and the other is *kainos* which means "renewed."

Both words for new are used in this verse and what Jesus was saying was that men put *brand new* wine into *renewed* wineskins. The *New American Standard Bible*[1] translates the verse ". . . but they put new wine into *fresh wine-*

---

[1]*New American Standard Bible* (La Habra: The Lockman Foundation, 1960, 1962, 1963, 1968, 1971, 1972, 1973, 1975, 1977), p. 7 of New Testament.

skins. . . ." Kenneth Wuest renders this verse *". . . But they put just-made wine into wineskins new in quality . . . ."*[2]

The impact of Jesus' statement comes through once we know that wineskins are renewed by being *rubbed with oil*. When they become soft and usable again, *wine* is poured in. Before we were born again, we were that old dried wineskin lying in the road, wounded by the devil and left as useless. But Jesus, our Good Samaritan, came along and rubbed us with *oil* (the New Birth), softened us up, made us usable again, then filled us with the *wine* (infilling of the Holy Spirit) of joy.

If you have been born again and taught that you have the Holy Spirit in His fullness right now, then it is the same as saying that a wineskin, once made soft with oil, has done what it was designed to do. No! It is prepared but not being used. If you are born again, you are *prepared*. Now, let the Lord *fill* you with the Holy Spirit.

---

[2] Kenneth S. Wuest, *The New Testament: An Expanded Translation* (Wm. B. Eerdmans, 1961), p. 21 of New Testament.

3
The Oil of the New Birth

Oil is used in the Word of God as a type and shadow, symbolizing the Holy Spirit in the New Birth. In Psalm 133 oil is used as a description of the unity of the New Birth. *"It is like the precious ointment* (anointing oil) *upon the head, that ran down upon the beard, even Aaron's beard: that went down to the skirts of his garments"* (v. 2).

The unity we have as believers is made possible by the one Spirit which made us one Body. (1 Cor. 12:13.) This oil of the New Birth began at the Head (Christ) on the day of Pentecost and ran down to the skirts of the garment (the Body of Christ). The oil continues to flow today and anoints each one who receives Jesus as his Lord. One day the last one will be added to the hem of the garment, the oil will flow over him, and Jesus will come back for a complete Body to fashion into His Bride. All the rooms in the inn will be full and the Good Samaritan will return for us.

Anointing with oil is a designation of rank. The highest in rank were always anointed with oil. Psalm 45:6-8 (also quoted in Heb. 1:8,9) tells us of the day when Jesus was anointed as King of Kings and Lord of Lords:

> Thy throne, O God, is for ever and ever: the sceptre of thy kingdom is a right sceptre.
>
> Thou lovest righteousness, and hatest wickedness: therefore God, thy God, hath anointed thee with the oil of gladness above thy fellows.
>
> All thy garments smell of myrrh, and aloes, and cassia, . . .

Jesus had just ascended into heaven from the pits of hell, where He had just conquered the devil, sin, and sickness. Although He still had the stench of corruption, God anointed Him with the oil of gladness above the level of angels. The smell of the anointing oil covered His head and garments. Once *we* receive the oil of the New Birth, we lose the smell of the kingdom of darkness and receive the sweet smelling savor of Jesus Himself. To God, the garments (Church) smell just like the Head (Jesus).

When Samuel was told by the Lord to go to the house of Jesse and anoint the new king of Israel, the most logical choices were the six brothers that Jesse brought out. They were all strong, tall, and good-looking. But God told Samuel that none of these was the right one. When Samuel inquired of any more sons, Jesse brought in David from the fields where he had been watching over sheep. David was the most illogical choice. He was dirty, smelled like the sheep, looked like the sheep, and was not as handsome to look upon as his other brothers. But God told Samuel that David was the one, and Samuel anointed him as the new king. (1 Sam. 16.)

The day that Jesus arose from hell and arrived in heaven, He was the most unlikely looking one to anoint as King of Kings. The angels such as Michael and Gabriel were a more obvious choice because of their dazzling beauty and strength. Jesus was a man with holes in His hands, holes in His feet, spear marks in His side, thorn holes in His brow, and stripes on His back. But, God by-passed all the angels and anointed Jesus and gave Him a name above every name. Thank God He did.

Since God anointed a man, then we too can be anointed, since we are men. Had God anointed an angel, we could never be born again and anointed with the oil of the Holy Spirit. When we are born again, we become a king with Jesus and are given dominion here on earth and joint heirship with Jesus of all things including the right to the use of His name, the name that causes even angels to bow — the name of *Jesus*.

Again, anointing with oil is a designation of rank. Every Christian became a king when he was born again and was anointed with the oil of the Holy Spirit. James 5:14 describes using oil in the local church as a point of contact for the sick to release faith for healing.

The elders of the church are to lay hands on and anoint with oil *"any sick among you."* This shows that divine healing is available to *all* who are born again because *oil* is used. The person who is sick has forgotten who he is in Christ and needs to be reminded. This is done by the anointing with oil. By seeing and feeling the oil, he remembers that he is a king and sickness is not part of his kingdom. His bill of rights (the Word) includes healing of every disease.

Oil is mentioned in Matthew 25 with the five wise virgins. The point of this parable is not that you must be filled with the Holy

Spirit and speak with tongues to enter heaven. The only element needed to enter the kingdom was *oil*. The *New Birth* is the only prerequisite for eternal life. The infilling of the Holy Spirit is never typified by oil, but by wine. Oil in the lamp of the virgins was used to light their way, and they lit them with fire.

On the day of Pentecost, *oil* was also poured out as we saw in Joel 2:24. Wine was poured out (Acts 2:13-15) and the evidence was seen when the disciples spoke in tongues. But on that day two other manifestations occurred: a sound from heaven as of rushing mighty wind, and also cloven tongues like as of *fire*. (Acts 2:2,3.) This was the manifestation of the *oil* filling the lamps (the bodies of the disciples). (See Heb. 1:7.)

Notice that the fire occurred before the speaking with tongues. Many around the world had believed on Jesus before the day of Pentecost including the 120 in the upper room. On this day though, the New Birth happened *worldwide*.

We so often limit the Holy Spirit to the upper room in Jerusalem, but one element of God flowed around the world that day: the *oil* of the *New Birth*. The disciples headed from the upper room that day to preach the message of *oil* and *wine*. To those who did not know Jesus as their Lord, both messages were preached — the New Birth and the infilling of the Holy Spirit. To those who had already believed on Jesus, the second work of the Spirit was taught. *Wine* was brought to those who had already received the *oil*.

4

The Wine of the Infilling

The second element that the Good
Samaritan poured into the wound was *wine*.
Notice that there was not one element but
two: the New Birth (oil) and infilling of the
Holy Spirit (wine). The Holy Spirit is capable
of doing more than one job just as you are.

Many limit the ministry of the Holy Spirit
today to salvation only and teach that you
received the fullness of the Spirit when you
were born again. It is true that the Holy Spirit
cannot be divided. You did not receive part
of the Holy Spirit when you were born again,
then at a later time receive the rest of Him.
The Holy Spirit is a personality and cannot
be divided.

But the Holy Spirit has more than one
ministry. He came to *live* in you at salvation,
but He desires to do a further work in you
by *filling* you with power for your daily life.
In other words, after giving *oil*, the Good
Samaritan wants to give you *wine*.

For too long we have given wine only one
meaning in the New Testament. We have

looked at this element only from the light of redemption and Jesus' work on the cross. It is true that wine in the communion elements speaks of the work of the blood of Jesus in redeeming us from our sins, but in the life *after* salvation, wine takes on a new meaning.

On the day of Pentecost, the Jews in the streets of Jerusalem thought that the disciples from the upper room were drunk on *new wine* because they heard them speaking in new tongues. Peter did not deny that they were drunk, but said *". . . these are not drunken, as ye suppose"* (Acts 2:15). These disciples had already believed on Christ and had been born again. Now they had received the fullness of the Spirit and had spoken with tongues.

In Ephesians 5:18, Paul tells the Ephesian saints: *"And be not drunk with wine, wherein is excess; but be filled with the Spirit."* Verse 19 goes on to say, *"Speaking to yourselves* (among yourselves) *in psalms and hymns and spiritual songs, singing and making melody in your heart to the Lord."* This sounds like the day of Pentecost. In both cases, the people were receiving an experience likened to being filled with wine. Also in both cases, the people had already been saved. Paul was writing to *saints*. Wine to excess in the natural produces a change in the person and so does being filled with the Spirit.

Isaiah 28:9-13 gives us the Old Testament parallel to Ephesians 5:18. The beginning of the chapter talks of kings who drink to excess and pass out on the tables. Then verses 11 and 12 say: *"For with stammering lips and another tongue will he speak to this people. To whom he said, This is the rest wherewith ye may cause the weary to rest; and this is the refreshing . . . ."* Wine to excess in the natural is wrong, but in the spiritual it brings rest and refreshing.

Anything to excess in the natural is wrong, but never in the spiritual. Be a spiritual glutton and never find a limit. When you think you've studied the Word of God enough, *study more.* When you think you've praised the Lord enough, *praise Him more.* Be not drunk on wine, but be *filled with the Spirit.*

5

What about Manifestations?

When people are born again, there may or may not be a manifestation. Some people "feel" saved, and others do not. I have traveled and spoken for many Full Gospel Business Men's Fellowship meetings and heard numerous testimonies. Many describe "feelings" or "sensations" which occurred when they were born again. This is great, and I do not doubt one word of these men at all. The trouble comes though, when we start to base salvation or any gift of God on other people's experiences.

Someone in a group or congregation might begin to doubt his own salvation because he did not "feel" what the speaker described. People must be educated by God's Word. With or without feeling, a person is born again when he acts according to scripture, believing that Jesus Christ is risen from the dead, and confessing with his mouth that Jesus Christ is now his Lord. (Rom. 10:9,10.)

33

One testimony I remember most came from a minister who said he had a headache *before* he was saved and still had a headache *after* he was saved. The New Birth is in the spirit, the inner man. Outward changes will come later as that changed man on the inside begins to affect the outer life.

The New Birth may or may not produce an outward manifestation in a person; the infilling of the Holy Spirit does. Being filled with the Holy Spirit brings on a manifestation, which is the evidence of speaking with tongues. *"Be filled with the Spirit; Speaking . . . ."* (Eph. 5:18,19). I bring up this point because of a growing controversy over whether a person needs to speak with tongues when filled with the Spirit.

Ironically it seems that some who expect a physical manifestation at the New Birth reject any manifestation of the infilling of the Holy Spirit. We need to stop expecting other people's experiences to happen to us and get back to what the Lord says in His Word. *". . . let God be true, but every man a liar"* (Rom. 3:4).

The Day of Pentecost —

ACTS 2:1-4

And when the day of Pentecost was fully come, they were all with one accord in one place.

And suddenly there came a sound from heaven as of a rushing mighty wind, and it filled all the house where they were sitting.

And there appeared unto them cloven tongues like as of fire, and it sat upon each of them.

And they were all filled with the Holy Ghost, and began to speak with other tongues, as the Spirit gave them utterance.

On the day of Pentecost there were three manifestations which accompanied the advent of the Holy Spirit on the hundred and twenty in the upper room. First, there was a sound from heaven like wind. Second, there were tongues like fire on each person; and finally, all hundred and twenty spoke with tongues or in languages which were unknown to them.

A minister who opposed this pentecostal experience said that if all charismatics want to be fully scriptural, they should not only speak in tongues when they are filled with the Spirit, but should also hear a sound of wind and see tongues of fire over their heads. I believe the answer to this argument will be self-explanatory as we go on to other scriptures.

In the *King James Bible*, the word *unknown* is usually used when referring to tongues. Many people have argued that because the word *unknown* is in italics (signifying that the word was not part of the original text — (see 1 Cor. 14:2,3,13,14) — that tongues were simply the person's ability to speak many foreign languages and preach the gospel to the heathen.

This use of the word *unknown* comes from the rest of the account of the day of Pentecost as seen in verses 6-11:

> Now when this was noised abroad, the multitude came together, and were confounded, because that every man heard them speak in his own language.

> And they were all amazed and marvelled, saying one to another, Behold, are not all these which speak Galilaeans?

And how hear we every man in our own tongue, wherein we were born? . . . .

. . . we do hear them speak in our tongues the wonderful works of God.

The argument that tongues were used by the Lord in the beginning of the church age to preach the gospel is stopped on the day it all began. On the day of Pentecost, when Peter *stopped* speaking with tongues and preached the gospel in the common language of the people, *then*, 3,000 people heard the message of salvation and were born again. (See vv. 14-41.)

Tongues were used to praise God and tell of His wonderful works. First Corinthians 14:2 says: *"For he that speaketh in an unknown tongue speaketh not unto men, but unto God. . . ."* "Tongues" is an assistance for the prayer life of the individual. Romans 8:26 states, *"Likewise the Spirit also helpeth our infirmities* (weaknesses): *for we know not what we should pray for as we ought."*

This verse refers to praying in the Holy Spirit, or in "unknown tongues." The reason why the word *unknown* is used is because the *SPEAKER* did not know the language he was speaking. First Corinthians 13:1 says that we can speak in the tongues of ". . . *men and angels.*" On the day of Pentecost the disciples spoke in the tongues of men because the Jews from every nation understood those who spoke the language of their country. At other times we can speak in the tongues of angels and the beings in the spirit realm can understand. But in either case, the *speaker* does not know what he is saying unless he interprets his tongue by the direction of the Holy Spirit. (I Cor. 14:5.)

I want to clear up one point before going any further. One misinterpretation of the Word exists today because of the use of the term "unknown tongues." Some people think that when they pray in the Spirit, the devil does not know what they are saying. This is not true. There is not one scripture to back that statement. You can only speak in the tongues of *men* or *angels,* and the devil knows *both*. The devil can understand every language of the world today, and he knows the languages of angels because he *is* one. But when Lucifer fell, he lost his anointing, his ability to understand *revelation knowledge.*

When you speak in tongues, the devil knows the words you are speaking, but not the *meaning.* Sinners today might tell you that they believe the Bible, but they are not saved, because they have not received the revelation of what the Bible is saying. They can read the Bible, but they do not understand it. The devils believe the Word, but they tremble (James 2:19) because they cannot receive the revelation of what the Word is saying. Satan might know the words you are speaking when you pray in the Spirit, but he cannot *understand* them.

A computer technician might talk of "software" and "electronic chips." I know what the words "soft," "ware," "electronic," and "chips" mean, but since I do not understand computer language, I would not know what "software" and "electronic chips" mean. The devil does not talk nor understand revelation language anymore. You speak revelation, because the Holy Spirit lives in you and guides your language. *"For if I pray in an [unknown] tongue, my spirit [by the Holy Spirit within me] prays . . . ."* (1 Cor. 14:14 AMP).[3]

The use of tongues during prayer edifies or builds up the one praying. Jude 20 says, *"But ye, beloved, **building up** yourselves on your most*

---

[3] *The Amplified Bible, New Testament* (La Habra: The Lockman Foundation, 1954, 1958) p. 265.

*holy faith, **praying in the Holy Ghost**."* The main use of tongues in your life is to enrich your prayer and praise life.

6

After Pentecost

The House of Cornelius —

Eight years after the day of Pentecost, the Gentiles were filled with the Holy Spirit in Cornelius' house. (Acts 10.)

> While Peter yet spake these words, the Holy Ghost fell on all them which heard the word.
>
> And they of the circumcision which believed were astonished, as many as came with Peter, because that on the Gentiles also was poured out the gift of the Holy Ghost.
>
> For they heard them *speak with tongues, and magnify God* . . . . (vv. 44-46).

There is no mention here of a sound from heaven like wind, nor of tongues as of fire over each of their heads. But there is the description of them speaking with tongues as the disciples did on the day of Pentecost.

The City of Ephesus —

Then twenty-one years after the outpouring of the Holy Spirit, Paul found some men who were saved some years before but had never been filled. Acts chapter 19 tells us that they were already born again because verse 1 refers to them as "certain disciples."

And it came to pass, that, while Apollos was at Corinth, Paul having passed through the upper coasts came to Ephesus: and finding certain disciples,

He said unto them, Have ye received the Holy Ghost *since ye believed?* And they said unto him, We have not so much as heard whether there be any Holy Ghost. . . .

And when Paul had laid his hands upon them, the Holy Ghost came on them; and they *spake with tongues, and prophesied* (vv. 1,2,6).

Notice again, that there is no mention of a sound from heaven as of wind, nor of tongues of fire over each person. But, the manifestation of tongues is mentioned here just as it was in chapters 2 and 10.

Second Corinthians 13:1 tells us, ". . . *In the mouth of two or three witnesses shall every word be established.*" In three scriptural references where the Holy Spirit was received, one manifestation was consistent — *speaking with tongues.* The Bible describes the sound of wind and tongues like fire as being displayed *only* at the initial out-pouring of the Holy Spirit on the day of Pentecost. The Holy Spirit is here today, and the evidence that He gives to us is a prayer and praise language to our Father in heaven.

In verse 6 it is stated that not only did the disciples at Ephesus speak with tongues, they also prophesied. Someone told me that he did not speak with tongues when he was filled with the Holy Spirit, but received discerning of spirits. He said that tongues was only one of a number of manifestations that might come with the Holy Spirit.

In regard to this, let me again refer to the house of Cornelius in Acts chapter 10. When the Gentiles from Caesarea were filled with the Holy Spirit, they spoke with tongues and *magnified God.* (v. 46.) How did the Jewish Christians know that these men magnified God? They must have been speaking in a known tongue. They must have been prophesying, because prophecy is an inspired utterance in a *known tongue.* The men who received the Holy Spirit in the house of Cornelius and the disciples at Ephesus both *spoke with tongues and prophesied.*

But in both scripture texts, notice which came *first.* It was *speaking with tongues.* They spoke with tongues first, *then* prophesied. The infilling of the Holy Spirit is the doorway into the gifts of the Spirit. If you receive discerning of spirits, prophecy, or any other gift, it will manifest itself after you speak with tongues.

The City of Samaria —

In the city of Samaria, the evangelist Philip preached a revival in which many came to the Lord Jesus Christ. This story has raised some questions as to whether a person needs to speak with tongues, because after Philip preached the gospel, Peter and John came to the city to pray for the people to receive the Holy Spirit, but no mention is ever made of the people receiving the manifestation of tongues. But I believe that after examining the following verses, we will come to the conclusion that the people in the city of Samaria did speak with tongues. Let's begin with Acts chapter 8, verses 5 through 7 and 12:

Then Philip went down to the city of Samaria, and preached Christ unto them. And the people with one accord gave heed unto those things which Philip spake, hearing and seeing the miracles which he did. For unclean spirits, crying with loud voice, came out of many that were possessed with them: and many taken with palsies, and that were lame, were healed . . .

But when they believed Philip preaching the things concerning the kingdom of God, and the name of Jesus Christ, they were baptized, both men and women.

It is obvious from these verses that the people at Samaria were born again. It is stated that they believed Philip, and that Philip preached Christ. In verses 14 through 17 we are told what happened when Jerusalem received the message of Samaria's revival:

Now when the apostles which were at Jerusalem heard that Samaria had received the word of God, they sent unto them Peter and John:

Who, when they were come down, prayed for them, that they might receive the Holy Ghost:

45

(For as yet he was fallen upon none of them: only they were baptized in the name of the Lord Jesus.)

Then laid they their hands on them, and they received the Holy Ghost.

From this part of the story, it can be seen that receiving the Holy Spirit was a separate act from salvation. Philip preached salvation and Peter and John preached of the filling of the Holy Spirit. In other words, Philip preached *oil*, and Peter and John preached *wine*.

A beautiful complement in ministries can also be seen in this account in Samaria. Philip was an evangelist and operated within the confines of his calling. He did not minister the Holy Spirit after he preached Christ. Peter and John were apparently used by the Lord in a specialized ministry, and through the laying on of their hands, people easily received the Holy Spirit.

We need to see that the Lord has called each one of us to a place within the Body of Christ and that we all have special gifts and callings. We are not called to be spiritual "Jacks of all trades." We need to recognize and make room for the ministries of others as the apostles did.

But now the real question arises, did the new converts at Samaria speak with tongues when they received the Holy Spirit? We are going to have to dig a little in the verses which follow this account, but I believe that you will have to agree that they did.

VERSES 18,19

And when Simon *saw* that through laying on of the apostles' hands the Holy Ghost was given, he offered them money,

Saying, Give me also this power, that on whomsoever I lay hands, he may receive the Holy Ghost.

If there were no manifestation when these converts received the Holy Spirit, then what did Simon *see*? You might say that he *saw* the Holy Spirit, but I remind you that the Holy Spirit is invisible. Simon must have seen some form of manifestation. If we are going to be consistent with other scriptures, we must assume that the people spoke in tongues. Another clue to this is found in Peter's reply to Simon.

VERSES 20,21

But Peter said unto him, Thy money perish with thee, because thou hast thought that the gift of God may be purchased with money.

Thou hast neither part nor lot in this matter; for thy heart is not right in the sight of God.

Peter told Simon that he had no part nor lot in the *matter*. In the margin of the old Scofield Bible there is a footnote about this word.[4] In the Greek this word is *logos*, which means "word." Peter said that Simon had no part nor lot in this utterance. I believe that the utterance was speaking with other tongues. What do you think?

[4]*The Scofield Reference Bible*, (New York: Oxford University Press, 1945) p. 1159.

7
Why Speak With Tongues?

After seeing that tongues is the evidence that a person has received the Holy Spirit, the next question which usually arises has to do with the actual speaking with tongues: Why should a person speak in a language that neither he nor many times anyone else can understand?

The fault with this argument is that it comes from human reasoning. We think that for something to do us any good, we must first of all *understand* it. Children are often this way. They have to be told to brush their teeth, take baths, and eat their vegetables. They would rather skip taking baths and brushing their teeth. They would also rather eat cake and candy instead of vegetables. We teach them properly because we know the importance of good habits. Children don't understand.

We are a lot like children when it comes to the spiritual. The Word of God says that speaking with tongues is important, but we want to *know* and *understand* first. Knowing and understanding comes under the area of the *mind*. But we are more than a body and mind, we are also a *spirit*. Since God is a Spirit, He communicates to us through our spirit. But the reverse is also true. *We communicate to God from our spirit.* The language of the spirit is different from that of the mind.

First Corinthians 14:14 says, *"For if I pray in an unknown tongue, my **spirit** prayeth, but my **understanding** is unfruitful."* Tongues are not to be understood by the *mind*, they are to be understood by *God*. I remind you that 1 Corinthians 14:2 says that speaking in tongues is speaking to *God*.

The language that you receive when you are filled with the Holy Spirit is a prayer and praise language. Remember that the disciples spoke with tongues and *magnified God*. The Jews on the day of Pentecost heard *"the wonderful works of God"* (Acts 2:11). First Corinthians 14:17 says that the one who speaks in tongues *"givest thanks well."* Jude 20 says that praying in the Holy Ghost (in tongues) *edifies* the one who prays: *"But ye, beloved, **building up** yourselves on your most holy faith, **praying** in the Holy Ghost."*

We are told in Romans 8:26,27 that the Holy Spirit has been given to us to assist in our prayer life:

Likewise the Spirit also helpeth our infirmities (*weaknesses*): for we know not what we should pray for as we ought: but the Spirit itself (*himself*) maketh intercession for us with groanings which cannot be uttered.

And he that searcheth the hearts knoweth what is the mind of the Spirit, because he maketh intercession for the saints according to the will of God.

The weakness spoken of here is not knowing what to pray for as we ought. The Spirit then helps us pray, and that is with other tongues, or as the King James says here, *"groanings which cannot be uttered."* Notice, the Spirit does not do our praying for us, but *helps*. He works together with us.

No more will you ever come from a time of prayer feeling "cheated." You will never again feel that your prayer was inadequate. We are limited in our own knowledge, and praying in tongues enables us to tap into the infinite knowledge and wisdom of God. God's will is given in His Word and by His

Spirit. Praying in tongues causes His Word to come alive in us and reveals His specific will to us. The Holy Spirit is given to us to help us overcome the limitations of the flesh.

When we begin to pray in that language of heaven, we suddenly move to a level of conversation equal with our Father's. First Corinthians 14:2 says that we *SPEAK TO GOD.* Imagine that! We are on the same level of conversation with the God of the universe.

Many times people have prayed to interpret their prayer language, and this is not wrong. First Corinthians 14:13 tells us that we may do this. But I do not believe that this is something we can *always* do. I do not believe that our finite minds could comprehend a conversation with God. It should then become easy to pray in faith when using our prayer language, because no unbelief can touch our mind as to what we're praying. Our *understanding is unfruitful.*

The beauty of praying in the Spirit, in other tongues, is that it is possible to pray no matter what you are doing. Since the mind is left free, you can pray in the Spirit and drive your car, work on the job, do housework, or even read your Bible. The scripture, *"Pray without ceasing"* (1 Thess. 5:17) now becomes a pleasant fulfillment instead of an impossible task.

Prayer for the New Birth

The Good Samaritan poured oil (symbolizing the New Birth) into the man's wounds first. It's important that you meet Jesus (*your* Good Samaritan) as your Savior. The Christian life begins by receiving the life of Jesus into your heart. If you have never done this, then I have a prayer (below) that I want you to say to God.

When you say the final "amen," you will be a part of God's family. All of God's rights, privileges, and assets will be yours.

Father, I believe in my heart that You raised Jesus from the dead for me. I now say with my mouth that Jesus is my Lord. I now have His life and His Spirit in me. From this time forward, my old life is dead. Everything is become new. I am born again. In Jesus' name, amen.

Prayer for the Infilling of the Holy Spirit

Since Jesus is now your Savior, He also wants to fill you with His Holy Spirit. The Good Samaritan Who gave you the oil, the New Birth, now wants to give you the wine, the infilling of the Holy Spirit.

Jesus says that He will give the Holy Spirit to those who ask. When you pray this prayer from a sincere heart, you will experience a new language rising from your spirit, deep inside you.

Your mind might be perplexed, but speak these words anyway. The Holy Spirit forms this language and your natural reason will have to step aside. When you say, "amen," the Holy Spirit will fill your spirit. Then begin to speak in other tongues.

Father, I ask You in faith for the gift of the Holy Spirit. You promised it to me, so I won't leave until I receive the blessing that is mine as Your child. I am now filled with Your Spirit and will

speak to You in other tongues. In Jesus'
name, amen.

Bob Yandian, Pastor of Grace Fellowship in Tulsa, Oklahoma, has an anointing and extensive teaching background that enables him to convey the uncompromised Word of God with an everyday practical clarity. Primarily, Bob ministers to students of the Word — fellow full-time ministers, congregational members, and Bible school students.

A graduate of Trinity Bible College, Bob studied under its director and founder, Charles Duncombe, a contemporary and companion of Smith Wigglesworth. Bob also studied Greek at Southwestern College in Oklahoma City.

In 1972 Bob began teaching regularly at Grace Fellowship where he was a founding member. In 1973 he began working for Kenneth Hagin Ministries as Tape Production Manager then, in 1977, for Rhema Bible Training Center as a teacher. Later he became Dean of Instructors. In 1980 he began pastoring Grace Fellowship.

Bob has taught and ministered throughout the United States and Canada, in South Africa, Guatemala, and the Philippines. He has spoken at numerous Full Gospel Businessmen's Fellowship International meetings; the Greater Pittsburgh Charismatic Conference; Bill Basansky's 1981, 1982, and 1983 jubilees; Salt Lake Institute of Religion (Mormon); and hosted the Local Church Seminar at Grace Fellowship.